BASIC DUAS

for children

Illustrated by Gurmeet
First published 2007
Reprinted 2013
© Goodword Books 2013

Islamic Vision Ltd.
434 Coventry Road, Small Heath
Birmingham B10 0UG, U.K.
Tel. 121-773-0137
Fax: 121-766-8577
e-mail: info@ipci-iv.co.uk
www.islamicvision.co.uk

Goodword Books
1, Nizamuddin West Market, New Delhi-110 013
Tel. 9111-4182-7083, 4652-1511
Fax: 9111-4565-1771
email: info@goodwordbooks.com
www.goodwordbooks.com

Printed in India

IB Publisher Inc.
81 Bloomingdale Rd, Hicksville
NY 11801, USA
Tel. 516-933-1000, Fax: 516-933-1200
Toll Free: 1-888-560-3222
email: info@ibpublisher.com
www.ibpublisher.com

BASIC DUAS
for children

Sr. Nafees Khan
Toronto, Canada

www.goodwordbooks.com

When we get up in the morning
The first thing that we say
Is to thank Allah Subhana wa Ta'ala
For giving us another day.

Dua Before Sleeping

اللَّهُمَّ بِاسْمِكَ اَمُوتُ وَاَحْيَا .

Allahumma bismika amootu wa ahyaa.

O Allah! With your name I die and live.

Dua After Waking up

اَلْحَمْدُ لِلّهِ الَّذِيْ اَحْيَانَا بَعْدَ مَا أَمَاتَنَا وَإِلَيْهِ النُّشُورُ .

Alhamdu lillahil ladhi ahyana ba'da maa amatana wa ilaihin nushoor.

All thanks to Allah who gave us life after having given death and (our) final return (on the day of Qiyaamah) is to Him.

Dua for Morning and Evening

بِسْمِ اللّهِ الَّذِي لَا يَضُرُّ مَعَ اِسْمِهِ شَيْءٌ فِي الْاَرْضِ وَلَا فِي السَّمَآءِ وَهُوَ السَّمِيْعُ الْعَلِيْمُ

Bismilla hil ladhi laa yadurru ma 'asmihi shaiun fil ardi walaa fis samaai wa huwas samee'ul 'aleem.

(I begin the day/ evening) in the name of Allah by whose name nothing on earth or in heavens can cause harm. He is the All-Hearing and the All-Knowing.

Enter the washroom while seeking His protection

Once you exit, it's time for another dua

Now do the wudu without wasting any water

Look up to the heavens and recite the shahada.

Dua for Entering the Toilet

اللّٰهُمَّ إِنِّيْ أَعُوْذُبِكَ مِنَ الْخُبُثِ وَالْخَبَائِثِ .

Allahumma innee a'udhu bika minal khubuthi wal khabaaithi

O Allah! I seek refuge with you from the bad male and female Jinns.

Dua on Leaving the Toilet

غُفْرَانَكَ

Ghufraa naka

I ask You (Allah) for forgiveness.

اَلْحَمْدُ لِلّٰهِ الَّذِيْ أَذْهَبَ عَنِّي الْأَذَى وَ عَافَانِي .

Alhamdu lillahil ladhi adhhaba 'annil adhaa wa 'aafaanee

All praise is for Allah who saved me from the harm and gave me relief.

Choose a clean place and spread the prayer rug
Always make intention to do your salaah.
After the Sunnah is over, the Fard is to be done
There's lot more reward when done in Jamaah.

Dua After the Adhan

اَللّٰهُمَّ رَبَّ هَذِهِ الدَّعْوَةِ التَّامَّةِ وَالصَّلَاةِ الْقَائِمَةِ آتِ مُحَمَّدَ نِالْوَسِيلَةَ وَالْفَضِيلَةَ وَابْعَثْهُ مَقَامًا مَحْمُودَ نِالَّذِي وَعَدْتَهُ، إِنَّكَ لَا تُخْلِفُ الْمِيْعَادِ.

Allahumma rabba haadhihid dawatit taammati was salaatil qaaimati aati Muhammada nil waseelata wal fadeelata wab'athhu maqamam mahmooda nil ladhi wa'attahu innaka laa tukhli fulmee'aad

O Allah, Lord of this perfect call and this everlasting salah, grant Muhammad (pbuh) (the right of) intercession and honour and raise him to the highest position which You have promised him. Surely, You do not break promises.

Dua Before Starting Salah

وَجَّهْتُ وَجْهِيَ لِلَّذِي فَطَرَ السَّمٰوَاتِ وَالْأَرْضَ حَنِيْفًا وَمَا أَنَا مِنَ الْمُشْرِكِيْنَ، إِنَّ صَلَاتِي وَنُسُكِي وَمَحْيَايَ وَمَمَاتِي لِلّٰهِ رَبِّ الْعٰلَمِيْنَ.

Wajjahtu wajhiya lil ladhee fataras samaawaati wal arda haneefaw wama ana minal mushrikeen.

I have turned my face firmly and truly towards Him Who created the heavens and the earth. And I am not of those who give partners to Him.

There are four more salaahs that are to be done
Zuhur, Asr, Maghrib and Isha with witr.
Follow the procedure for the morning prayer
Remember, there are only two rakaahs for Fajr.

10

Dua al Qunoot

اَللّٰهُمَّ اِنَّا نَسْتَعِيْنُكَ وَنَسْتَغْفِرُكَ (وَنَتُوْبُ اِلَيْكَ) وَنُثْنِيْ عَلَيْكَ الْخَيْرَ (وَنَشْكُرُكَ) وَلَا نَكْفُرُكَ

وَنَخْلَعُ وَنَتْرُكُ مَنْ يَّفْجُرُكَ اَللّٰهُمَّ اِيَّاكَ نَعْبُدُ وَلَكَ نُصَلِّيْ وَنَسْجُدُ وَالَيْكَ نَسْعَى وَنَحْفِدُ،

وَنَخْشَى عَذَابَكَ (الْجِدَّ) وَنَرْجُوْ رَحْمَتَكَ اِنَّ عَذَابَكَ (الْجِدَّ) بِالْكُفَّارِ مُلْحِقٌ.

Allahumma inna nasta'eenuka wa nastaghfiruka (wa natuubu ilaika) wa nusnee 'alaikal khair, (was nash kuruka) walaa nakfuruka wa nakhla'u wa natruku main yafjuruka, allahumma iyyaka na'budu wa laka nusallee wa nasjudu wa ilaika nas'aa wa nahfidu, wa nakhsha 'azaabaka (ul jidda) wa narju rahmataka inna 'azabaka(ul jidda) bil kuffari mulhiq.

O Allah we seek help from You and ask for Your forgiveness (and turn towards You) We rely on You. We praise You for all the good things. We thank You and are not ungrateful to You. We part and break off from all who disobey You.

O Allah, You alone we worship , and to You do we pray and prostrate before You and to You do we flee, we fear Your severe punishment and hope for Your mercy. Your severe punishment is to be given out to the unbelievers.

We must praise Allah by glorifying Him
It is quite easy and is known as Tasbeeh
Subhanallah, Alhamdulillah and Allahuakbar
These are to be said thirty three times each.

Tasbeeh (Glorification)

سُبْحَانَ اللّهِ

Subhanallah   33 times

Glory to Allah

Allah is pure.

الْحَمْدُ لِلّهِ

Alhamdulillah   33 times

All praise to Allah

اللّهُ اَكْبَرُ

Allahu Akbar   33 or 34 times

Allah is the greatest

Dua After tasbeeh

لَا إِلَهَ إِلَّا اللّهُ وَحْدَهُ لَا شَرِيك لَهُ، لَهُ الْمُلْكُ وَلَهُ الْحَمْدُ يُحْيِي وَيُمِيتُ بِيَدِهِ الْخَيْرُ وَهُوَ عَلَى كُلِّ شَيْءٍ قَدِيرٌ.

Laa ilaha illallahu wahdahu laa shareeka lahu, lahul mulku wa lahul hamdu yuhyee wa yumeetu be yadihil khairu wa huwa 'ala kulle shai in qadeer.

There is no God but Allah, He is one and has no partner, to Him belongs the Universe and Praise, Giver of life and death; He is the Living who does not die. In His hand is all good, and He is powerful over everything.

13

Be first in saying Salaam to everyone around

The one who greets first earns extra ajr.

Now we are ready for our morning meal

Start and end in His name, it's best to eat together.

Dua Upon Meeting a Muslim

اَلسَّلَامُ عَلَيْكُمْ وَرَحْمَةُ اللّهِ وَبَرَكَاتُهُ.

Assalaamu alaikum wa rahmatul laahi wa barakaatuhu

Peace be upon you and the Mercy of Allah and His Blessings.

14

وَعَلَيْكُمُ السَّلَامُ وَرَحْمَةُ اللهِ وَبَرَكَاتُهُ.

Wa 'alaikumus salaamu wa rahmatul laahi wa barakaatuhu

And peace be upon you and the Mercy of Allah and His Blessings.

Dua Before Eating

بِسْمِ اللهِ

a) **Bismillah**

In the name of Allah   or

بِسْمِ اللهِ وَعَلَى بَرَكَةِ اللهِ.

b) **Bismillahi wa 'ala baraka tillaahi**

In the name of Allah and upon the Blessings of Allah.

Dua After Eating

اَلْحَمْدُ لِلهِ الَّذِي اَطْعَمَنَا وَسَقَانَا وَجَعَلَنَا مِنَ الْمُسْلِمِينَ.

Alhamdu lillahil ladhi at'amana wa saqaana waja'alana minal muslimeen.

All praises is for Allah who has fed us and given us drink and who had made us Muslims.

15

Leave for school by putting trust in your Lord

Pray for knowledge and to stay on the right track

Always work hard, be fair, kind and truthful

Respect your teachers and never talk back.

Dua When Leaving Home

بِسْمِ اللهِ تَوَكَّلْتُ عَلَى اللهِ.

Bismillahee tawakkaltu 'alal laahi

In the name of Allah, I trust Allah.

Dua on Boarding a Car or Other Vehicle

سُبْحَانَ الَّذِيْ سَخَّرَ لَنَا هَذَا وَ مَا كُنَّا لَهُ مُقْرِنِيْنَ وَ إِنَّا اِلَى رَبِّنَا لَمُنْقَلِبُوْنَ.

Subhanal ladhi sakhkhara lana haadha wama kunna lahu muqrineen wa inna ila rabbina la munqaliboon.

Glory be to Allah, who has brought this (car, vehicle, etc.) under our control though we were unable to control it. Surely, we are to return to our Lord.

Dua While Entering Home

اللَّهُمَّ اِنِّيْ اَسْئَلُكَ خَيْرَ الْمَوْلَجِ وَخَيْرَ الْمَخْرَجِ، بِسْمِ اللهِ وَلَجْنَا وَبِسْمِ اللهِ خَرَجْنَا، وَعَلَى اللهِ رَبِّنَا تَوَكَّلْنَا.

Allahumma innee as'aluka khairal mawlaji wa khairal makhraji, bismillahi walajna wa bismillahi kharajna, wa 'alal lahi rabbana tawakkalna

O Allah, I ask you the blessings of entering and leaving. With Allah's name we enter and with Allah's name we leave and we trust our Lord.

Dua to Increase Knowledge

رَبِّ زِدْنِيْ عِلْماً

Rabbee zidnee 'ilma

O my Lord, increase my knowledge.

17

When you're lucky to wear nice new things

Which could be a dress or a pair of new shoes.

Thank Allah for giving you these gifts

For without His will nothing comes true!

18

Dua for Wearing New Things

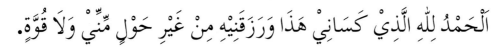

ٱلْحَمْدُ لِلّهِ الَّذِيْ كَسَانِيْ هَذَا وَرَزَقَنِيْهِ مِنْ غَيْرِ حَوْلٍ مِّنِّيْ وَلَا قُوَّةٍ.

a)Alhamdu lillahil ladhi kasaani haadha warazaqa neehi min ghairi howlim minnee walaa quwwatin

All praise is for Allah who gave me this to wear and gave it to me without any strength and ability on my part.

ٱلْحَمْدُ لِلّهِ

b) Alhamdu lillah   3times

All praise is for Allah

ٱلْحَمْدُ لِلّهِ رَبِّ الْعَالَمِيْنَ.

c) Alhamdu lillahi rabbil 'aalameen

All praise is for Allah the Lord of the worlds.

When someone does you a favour

It should be appreciated readily

When you thank others well

You also make Allah happy.

Dua to Thank Allah

اَلْحَمْدُ لِلّهِ الَّذِيْ بِعِزَّتِهِ وَجَلَالِهِ تَتِمُّ الصَّالِحَاتُ.

Alhamdu lilla hil ladhi be izzatihee wa jalaalihee tatimmus saalihaat

All praise is for Allah by whose Honour and Majesty, good deeds are accomplished.

Dua to Thank Parents

رَبِّ ارْحَمْهُمَا كَمَا رَبَّيَانِيْ صَغِيْرًا

Rabbir hum humaa kamaa rabba yaanee sagheera

My Lord, have mercy on them just as they brought me up when I was young

Dua to Thank People

جَزَاكَ اللّهُ خَيْرًا (to a boy)
Jazaakallahu khairan

جَزَاكِ اللّهُ خَيْرًا (to a girl)
Jazaakillahu khairan

May Allah give you a better reward.

An istighfaar should be done on a daily basis

As our beloved Prophet (pbuh) used to do

He said it several times each and every day

It is a Sunnah that we must follow too!

Istighfaar

اَسْتَغْفِرُ اللّٰهَ

a) astaghfirul laaha
I seek Allah's forgiveness.

اَسْتَغْفِرُ اللّٰهَ الَّذِيْ لَاۤ اِلٰهَ اِلَّا هُوَ الْحَيُّ الْقَيُّوْمُ وَاَتُوْبُ اِلَيْهِ.

b) astaghfirul laahal ladhi laa ilaaha illaa huwal haiyyul qaiyoomu wa atubu ilaihi.

I beg Allah's forgiveness, the One besides whom, none has the right to be worshipped except He. The Everliving, the Everlasting , and I turn to Him in repentence.

Saiyyidul Istighfaar

اللّٰهُمَّ أَنْتَ رَبِّي، لَا إِلٰهَ إِلَّا أَنْتَ، خَلَقْتَنِي وَأَنَا عَبْدُكَ، وَأَنَا عَلَى عَهْدِكَ وَوَعْدِكَ مَا اسْتَطَعْتُ أَعُوذُ بِكَ مِنْ شَرِّ مَا صَنَعْتُ، أَبُوءُ لَكَ بِنِعْمَتِكَ عَلَيَّ، وَأَبُوءُ بِذَنْبِي، فَاغْفِرْ لِي، فَإِنَّهُ لَا يَغْفِرُ الذُّنُوبَ إِلَّا أَنْتَ.

c) Allahumma anta rabbi, laa ilaha illa anta, khalaqtani wa ana abduka, wa ana 'ala ahdika wa wa'dika mastata'tu, a'oodhu bika min sharri ma sana'tu, aboou laka beni'matika 'alaiyya wa aboou be zambee, faghfir lee fa innahoo laa yaghfirudh dhunooba illa anta.

O Allah, You are my Lord. None has the right to be worshipped except You. You created me and I am Your servant, and I abide to Your covenant and promise as best as I can. I take refuge in You from the evil that I have done. I acknowledge your favour upon me and I acknowledge my faults (sin). So forgive me, for none can forgive sins except You.

 The author Sr. Nafees Khan earned her Bachelor of Art's degree at Aligarh Muslim University in India and completed her teacher's training in Canada. Her career spans over thirty years as a teacher in elementary public schools. She has been an active member of the Toronto Muslim community since 1967. She has a special interest in the education of Muslim children and played a key role in the establishment of two full-time Islamic schools, Islamic Foundation School and Al Falah School in Toronto. Sr. Nafees served as Principal at both schools. Her other books are "Prophet of Peace" and "Allah's Zoo".